Samuel French Acting Edition

George Washington's Teeth

by Mark St. Germain

SAMUELFRENCH.COM   SAMUELFRENCH.CO.UK

Copyright © 2019 by Mark St. Germain
All Rights Reserved

GEORGE WASHINGTON'S TEETH is fully protected under the copyright laws of the United States of America, the British Commonwealth, including Canada, and all other countries of the Copyright Union. All rights, including professional and amateur stage productions, recitation, lecturing, public reading, motion picture, radio broadcasting, television and the rights of translation into foreign languages are strictly reserved.

ISBN 978-0-573-70793-3

www.SamuelFrench.com
www.SamuelFrench.co.uk

FOR PRODUCTION ENQUIRIES

UNITED STATES AND CANADA
Info@SamuelFrench.com
1-866-598-8449

UNITED KINGDOM AND EUROPE
Plays@SamuelFrench.co.uk
020-7255-4302

Each title is subject to availability from Samuel French, depending upon country of performance. Please be aware that *GEORGE WASHINGTON'S TEETH* may not be licensed by Samuel French in your territory. Professional and amateur producers should contact the nearest Samuel French office or licensing partner to verify availability.

CAUTION: Professional and amateur producers are hereby warned that *GEORGE WASHINGTON'S TEETH* is subject to a licensing fee. Publication of this play(s) does not imply availability for performance. Both amateurs and professionals considering a production are strongly advised to apply to Samuel French before starting rehearsals, advertising, or booking a theatre. A licensing fee must be paid whether the title(s) is presented for charity or gain and whether or not admission is charged. Professional/Stock licensing fees are quoted upon application to Samuel French.

No one shall make any changes in this title(s) for the purpose of production. No part of this book may be reproduced, stored in a retrieval system, or transmitted in any form, by any means, now known or yet to be invented, including mechanical, electronic, photocopying, recording, videotaping, or otherwise, without the prior written permission of the publisher. No one shall upload this title(s), or part of this title(s), to any social media websites.

For all enquiries regarding motion picture, television, and other media rights, please contact Samuel French.

MUSIC USE NOTE

Licensees are solely responsible for obtaining formal written permission from copyright owners to use copyrighted music in the performance of this play and are strongly cautioned to do so. If no such permission is obtained by the licensee, then the licensee must use only original music that the licensee owns and controls. Licensees are solely responsible and liable for all music clearances and shall indemnify the copyright owners of the play(s) and their licensing agent, Samuel French, against any costs, expenses, losses and liabilities arising from the use of music by licensees. Please contact the appropriate music licensing authority in your territory for the rights to any incidental music.

IMPORTANT BILLING AND CREDIT REQUIREMENTS

If you have obtained performance rights to this title, please refer to your licensing agreement for important billing and credit requirements.

GEORGE WASHINGTON'S TEETH premiered at Florida Repertory Theatre in Fort Myers, Florida on April 24, 2018. The performance was directed by Abigail Zealey Bess, with set design by Jim Hunter, lighting design by Annmarie Duggan, costume design by Alice Neff, and sound design by John Kiselica. The production stage manager was Amy L. Massari. The cast was as follows:

HESTER BUNION	Carrie Lund
ANN MATHER	Liz Abbott
EDIE PLOTZ	Viki Boyle
JESS WILDER	Jackie Rivera
LOUISA TYE	Patricia R. Floyd
MAYOR RONALD RICE / BIG JIM / ANNOUNCER	Jason Parrish

CHARACTERS

HESTER BUNION – President of the New Bunion Historical Society and its oldest member. Descendant of New Bunion's 1705 founder, Sampson Bunion. White.

ANN MATHER – Wife of Jayden Mather, wealthy partner in the Mather and Mather investment firm. Stylish, attractive. One-time trophy wife. White.

EDIE PLOTZ – Florist. Narcoleptic. Knows every birth, death, and affair in town. Middle-aged. White.

JESS WILDER – College-aged. Real-world smart. White.

LOUISA TYE – Descendant of one of New Bunion's first settlers. Scholar. Black.

MAYOR RONALD RICE, BIG JIM, ANNOUNCER – Voice-overs.

SETTING

New Bunion Historical Society Museum, New Bunion, New England

TIME

The Present

(New Bunion Town Hall. As lights rise, **MAYOR RONALD RICE**'s voice is heard on a sound system that should be retired. Like the mayor.)*

MAYOR. *(Voice-over.)* The Commissioners of New Bunion want to thank the VFW for their memorial plaque honoring all New Bunionites who gave their lives for our country. We also wish Calvin Bickford a speedy recovery after seeing his name accidentally inscribed.
And, finally, excitement mounts for our first Latvian Song and Dance Festival.
Please contact Valdis Valters at Valters' Chicken Sexing if you are from, visited, or know anyone from Latvia.

*(Enter through the house the well-dressed **ANN MATHER**; the nervous, eager to please **EDIE PLOTZ**; and the authoritative **HESTER BUNION**, arms crossed with disapproval. There are chairs or a bench behind them.)*

Next up we'll hear from the longtime president of the New Bunion Historical Society, Hester Bunion.

ANN. Actually, Mr. Mayor, as the society's board secretary, it's my duty to respond to your registered letter of June 28.

MAYOR. *(Voice-over, a little too pleased to see her.)* Ann! Wonderful! It's always a treat to see you!

HESTER. *(A whisper loud enough to be heard.)* Watch him: that man's as slippery as a French kiss.

EDIE. *(Nervous "shush.")* Hester!

ANN. Mr. Mayor –

MAYOR. *(Voice-over.)* "Ronnie," Ann. Please.

---

*Town Hall site can be played in front of curtain

ANN. Ronnie, we strongly protest your huge cut in our budget, especially considering the incredibly large sum you just authorized for building the doggy water park.

MAYOR. *(Voice-over.)* It's in partnership with the Canine Olympics.

ANN. As far as addressing the first point in your letter: Yes, our museum's attendance is down. But that's beyond our control.

EDIE. Acts of God.

HESTER. A Vengeful God.

ANN. Our Fall exhibit "The Leaves of New Bunion" was cut short by an attack of spider mites –

HESTER. Only seven leaves left.

ANN. Leaves eaten by the Asian ladybugs brought in to eat the spider mites.

EDIE. I am *so* sorry.

ANN. We had no choice but to cancel the exhibit. But on a positive note, museum walk-in visitors have nearly doubled.

EDIE. And less than half of them wanted to use the facilities.

(HESTER nudges EDIE to keep quiet.)

ANN. *(Departing from notes.)* Ronnie, face it, your proposal to relocate the museum is just plain wrong. Why should we move out of the old firehouse?

HESTER. Especially for the fire department? They wanted their fancy new building and they got it! Who told them to buy another fire truck? They'll only use it in the Fourth of July parade and we all know it!

EDIE. *(Impassioned.)* Every town has fires! How many have New Bunion History! How...many... *(Gasps for air.)*

ANN. *(Concerned.)* Deep breath, Edie.

HESTER. Sit down, girl!

EDIE. Why in the... How can you. It's so... Oh boy.

(EDIE freezes, then falls backward into the seat behind her. Commotion.)

MAYOR. *(Voice-over.)* Call an ambulance!

ANN. She'll be fine.

HESTER. *(To* **EDIE.***)* Forgot your pills again?

ANN. Edie has a form of narcolepsy. Excitement rushes the blood to her head. It's never for long.

> (**EDIE** *shakes it off, opens her eyes, looks toward Heaven.*)

EDIE. Lord?

HESTER. He still doesn't want you.

ANN. Don't close the doors on history. Our museum is about more than maps and muskets. It's about love for our town and our country.

> *(Sound of weak applause.* **HESTER** *glares at the audience and the applause immediately grows louder.)*

MAYOR. *(Voice-over.)* Ladies: we have no intention of putting you out on the street. You'll be happy to know your museum will be relocated in a space nearly twice the size you have now.

EDIE. Huzzah! Thank you, Mayor! I am so excited... *(Starts to freeze.)*

ANN. *(Caution.)* Deep breath!

EDIE. *(Takes deep breath.)* Good to go.

HESTER. *(Wary.)* Where is this space you're talking about?

MAYOR. *(Voice-over.)* Once the asbestos is cleared, you will have the full basement of the Golden Years Social Club.

ANN. *(Horrified.)* The senior center?

EDIE. NO!

> (**EDIE** *sways and falls backward into her seat again.*)

HESTER. *(Furious.)* Now you listen to me, Ronnie Rice! You were a good-for-nothing when I taught you in fifth grade and you're good for even less now! You couldn't spell "history" let alone learn any – you were too busy getting locked in the closet by the other kids for being the class weasel!

ANN. Hester, I'll handle this –

HESTER. We are not moving to Geezer Gardens! I won't have those dinosaurs shuffling through our museum and leaving their whiffs of Depends.

EDIE. *(Waking.)* Lord?

HESTER. I'M TALKING!

(**EDIE** *passes out again.*)

ANN. Mr. Mayor, Council, there has to be another solution.

HESTER. *(A new idea.)* There is. We want to buy the old firehouse.

(**EDIE** *wakes.*)

MAYOR. *(Voice-over.)* What?

ANN. No!

EDIE. Hester!

HESTER. Give us six months and we'll raise whatever it takes. Contributions, grants, loans, anything that will free us from you Washington wannabees.

ANN. Hester, this is something the executive committee needs to vote on!

HESTER. We're it! I vote "Yea"! You?

ANN. We can't take on something like this.

HESTER. It's "Yea" or "Nay" –

ANN. "Nay"!

HESTER. *(To* **EDIE**, *who's getting up.)* Your call, girl! Do we buy the building or not? What say you?

ANN. Sit down, first.

EDIE. *(She does.)* I think the senior center's nice enough. People could visit after they play Bingo.

HESTER. Sure. Then we can lead them down the stairs singing "The Wheels on the Bus."

ANN. Just say "no," Edie.

HESTER. You want to be the reason for the eradication of 200 years of history?

EDIE. We have nothing in our treasury!

ANN. Negative numbers!

HESTER. Remember the words of Thomas Paine: "We will hang together or we will hang separately."

ANN. That was Benjamin Franklin.

HESTER. AFTER Paine.

(To **EDIE.***)* What'll it be, girl, yea or nay?

MAYOR. Miss Plotz?

EDIE. I move we postpone the vote –

ANN. Seconded.

HESTER. I object.

EDIE. I think... My vote... We should –

*(***EDIE** *falls back.)*

ANN. *(Frustrated.)* And she's off.

HESTER. *(Defiant.)* I heard a "Yea."

(Lights down on Town Hall.)

BIG JIM. *(Voice-over.)* Wake up, New Bunion! Big Jim coming to you on WNBN. It looks like war between the mayor and our historical society. After the town council voted to move the society they countered with a proposal to buy their current home. So, head to the Museum Membership Drive tonight, or, join the mayor for the Official Wet Down of our new Husky 3 fire truck, with all the beer you can drink.

(Lights up on the New Bunion Museum. It's small and cluttered, an antique itself.)

(There are three doors: the front entrance, the rear exit, and the "staff only" storeroom.)

(Shelves and cases of exhibits line the walls, and there is a glass display case somewhere close to the middle of the room. Displays range from a mounted bear's head to a large chair made with moose antlers.)

(A Civil War cannon sits before a wall of weapons: a colonial musket, a western gun

belt with a Colt .45, a WWI rifle with bayonet, and a WWII machine gun.)

(**HESTER** *and* **EDIE** *set up folding chairs.*)

EDIE. You'll never believe who Simon Henkel's newest conquest is.

HESTER. Molly Strutt?

EDIE. She was last month.

HESTER. Who?

EDIE. Merry Hoff.

HESTER. The reverend's wife?

EDIE. Her prayers were answered. And Simon's pulling out the big guns to impress her. He had us send her a Valentino Orchid Basket. He never sent Lena more than our Dandelion Delight.

HESTER. Is there anything going on you don't know about?

EDIE. When you're town florist you get first word of every birth, death, and fornication.

(**ANN** *enters.*)

ANN. That's enough chairs. We haven't had that many people here since our "Syphilis and the Civil War" exhibit.

EDIE. Tonight we might. *The Patriot* published my press release calling for new members and I put posters in the lobby of Whale-Ho Realty and the nail parlor.
(*Confiding.*) I don't think Cutiecles is doing well. The nail girls keep getting younger and their free massages last longer.

ANN. I've never seen so many men in town with buffed nails. Stop with the chairs, Hester!

EDIE. People will come. You'll see.

ANN. And if they do come, then what? We hike up their dues to ten thousand a year?

HESTER. I've got a battle plan.

ANN. Can you share it?

HESTER. When we get to "New Business."

ANN. Then let's get there. Start the meeting.

EDIE. It's only seven oh five. Shouldn't we wait?

ANN. Not unless you want to flag down cars.

> (**HESTER** *climbs up the stairs to stand in a 250-year-old, fire-scarred pulpit.*)

HESTER. The five hundred and seventy-sixth meeting of the New Bunion Historical Society will come to order. Roll call.

ANN. Come on, Hester! We voted to discontinue role calls!

EDIE. Hester vetoed our vote.

HESTER. Ellie Elkton.

EDIE. Sick. Phlebitis.
(Confiding.) Her legs look like a map of the Blue Mountains; it's so sad.

HESTER. *(Cutting her off.)* Thomas Tinker?

EDIE. Sick.

ANN. Of coming.

HESTER. Wyman Twill?

EDIE. Deceased. The Odd Fellows got him a grave blanket in the shape of a Studebaker. Extra large.

HESTER. Melody Sweet?

EDIE. Living with her son, Ruddy.
*(To **ANN**.)* You remember Ruddy – he was the first Boy Scout to get a merit badge in Piercing.

HESTER. Franklin Dunphy?

EDIE. Florida.

HESTER. Rose Stanley?

EDIE. Dead.

HESTER. Moe Fletcher?

ANN. Dead and in Florida. I move we conclude role call.

EDIE. Seconded. It's just too depressing.

HESTER. Suck it up. Do we have a report from the membership committee?

ANN. Look around the room!

EDIE. *(Getting upset.)* I really did all I could –

HESTER. No waterworks!

EDIE. I even visited the nursing home. They only travel for evacuations.

HESTER. Fine. Let's move to the budget.

EDIE. Since we only have one night, I won't detail all our overdue bills. But at the top of the list is gas and electric.

ANN. What's the due date?

EDIE. August first –

ANN. That's not so bad.

EDIE. Of last year. Not to worry. I called them and they won't turn off power until the sixth.

ANN. That's next week!

EDIE. Truthfully, Ann, I was hoping we'd get the Mather Trust donation before then.

HESTER. *(To **ANN**.)* What's the story? Is your husband writing a check or not?

ANN. *(A slight hesitation.)* I haven't had a chance to talk with Jayden, he's been buried at work.

HESTER. Good! Guilt! That means a bigger donation. Just remind him that his family has supported us for half a century. He doesn't want to look like the first Mather cheapskate. Can you shake him down tonight?

ANN. I'm not sure. He's been staying at our apartment in the city – it saves commuting time.

EDIE. We still have our grant to the state cultural council.

HESTER. I sent it off Monday, Special Delivery. Their deadline's tomorrow.

ANN. We can't depend on the council. They didn't support us at all last year.

EDIE. I don't know why they didn't fund our left-handed doorknob exhibit.

ANN. Hester, can we move on to your battle plan?

EDIE. *This* is exciting!

HESTER. We, of all people, should realize that the solutions of the present can be found in the past. If we want to win this war, what could be more fitting than the Three Point Mock Flanking Maneuver used by every leader from Hannibal to Patton.

ANN. The "Three Point Mock Flanking Maneuver"?

EDIE. Does this involve horses? Mr. Ed gave me nightmares.

HESTER. No horses. We are being attacked on three sides: Apathy, Poverty, and Bureaucracy. Flank one: Apathy – how many residents of New Bunion have ever set foot in here? How many even know we exist?

ANN. That's true.

EDIE. Don't say that! Every year we have the entire grammar school here for New Bunion Day.

ANN. Edie, I play tennis with the president of the school board. She told me New Bunion Day holds the record for parents phoning their kids in sick. Over seventy-five percent of the student body stayed home last year.

EDIE. It was flu season.

ANN. A *one day* flu season? Even the kids who came to school had to be threatened with no lunch for a week if they didn't get on the bus. And half of *them* held out. Who wants to come here year after year to watch three old ladies in granny costumes serve venison pudding, shouting, "Hands off the guns"?! Our biggest draw is the arrowhead display, and we have to borrow that from South Salem because no tribe ever wanted to settle here.

EDIE. Maybe we should go back to the Mohegan Sun casino and ask them to loan us their Native American displays.

HESTER. Absolutely not. They'll pull a switcheroo like they did last time. "Pocahontas Poker"? "Custer's Last Slots"?

ANN. We should have thrown them out the minute they unloaded their "Trail of Tears" craps table.

EDIE. I thought it was educational.

HESTER. Really? Should we ask Boston Bourbon to pitch in? Free shots for the kiddies followed by a half in the bag sack race?

ANN. Listen to us. We can't even agree on the first flank of your plan. Can we once be realistic? We don't have the money to keep the lights on, let alone buy this building. And then there's your membership criteria: How can you insist it's limited to families who at least, quote, "knew someone who knew someone on the Mayflower"?

HESTER. We take their word for it. Or we don't.

ANN. While you, as president, make that decision.

HESTER. As my mother did and her mother did before her. It's called "Tradition." My forefather Sampson Bunion founded this town!

> (**ANN** and **EDIE** don't even try to conceal their apathy.)

And wrote our charter sitting in that very chair he shot this moose for.

EDIE. Ohhh. I thought they shot *him* in the moose chair.

HESTER. Sampson wasn't just writing for the first settlers, he was writing for all of us who came after. Can't we ever leave anything alone without changing it for the worst? Do you think our forefathers would have allowed a Bread Line on Main Street? A drug dealer's den? You can't even buy a book in town anymore – you have to drive out to the Pilgrim Mall for one of those plastic books you can electrocute yourself with.

This is not the town Sampson founded. The town George Washington, stayed in not one night not two, but three nights! He knew what America *should be*, and that's why we're here, to make people remember that!

ANN. *(Gently.)* Hester, it's not a Bread Line it's a Panera Bread. There are no drug dealers, that's a Walgreens drive-through. And George Washington stayed here only two nights.

HESTER. Three.

ANN. Two.

HESTER. I know how many nights he stayed!

ANN. *(Gently.)* Hester? You're worried about this museum and you're under a lot of pressure.

HESTER. You think I don't know that?

ANN. I'm just saying, it's easy to get confused.

HESTER. What's your point, Edie?

ANN. "Ann."

EDIE. I'm Edie.

> (**HESTER** *glares at her.*)

But you can call me "Ann."

HESTER. Are you trying to embarrass me?

ANN. No! Everyone gets confused sometimes.

EDIE. I forgot to get dressed once before I did yard work. I was wondering why raking leaves drew such a crowd.

ANN. Hester, you've lived here all your life, sometimes you want to remember the past the way you wish it was. We all want good things to stay the same. But they always change, like seasons do.

HESTER. Is Mother Nature finished?

ANN. Not yet. Maybe we're holding on here for the wrong reasons. We have to stop looking back and look at our future. I'm sorry, Hester. I don't see one.

HESTER. So what do you want to do? Just give up?

ANN. I want to sit down with the mayor and work out a compromise. Take the exhibits we have and install them in the library so people can still see them.

EDIE. She's right, Hester. Maybe we've been fooling ourselves about people's interest. Look at the American Revolution reenactors! They use our grounds every year and that thug, Humphrey Hodkins, still refuses to help us with publicity.

ANN. Edie, he was right. Colonists can't wear museum t-shirts.

HESTER. And give it a rest with Humphrey. Admit it, you're sweet on the guy and you have been since he threw you in the dumpster in second grade.

ANN. Can we forget Humphrey Hodkins?

EDIE. I have! *(Still griping.)* He doesn't even play a colonist. He plays King George, just for the crown.

ANN. Edie! Should we close the museum or not?

EDIE. Hester? I don't want to hurt your feelings, and I know how hard you and your family have worked all these years, but Ann's right. We should donate our collections to the library. Maybe even more people will see them there.

HESTER. And what happens when the library's gone, too?

> *(Knock on the door, which opens.* **JESSICA WILDER** *enters, a young woman with a fondness for black leather and tattoos. She's smoking a cigarette.)*

JESS. *(Thinks she has the wrong place.)* Sorry. I didn't know this was the senior center.

HESTER. It's not! We are the New Bunion Historical Society. And we do not allow smoking.

> *(***JESS*** spits in one hand, then grinds the cigarette out on it.)*

JESS. Not a problem. You're the guys I'm looking for. I thought there was a meeting at seven?

ANN. You're looking at it. Can we help you?

JESS. You want, like, new members, right?

EDIE. Right!

JESS. Awesome. Sign me up.

> *(The women look at each other.)*

EDIE. Oh my! She's a mitzvah!

ANN. A "*mitzvah*"?

EDIE. We did a huge Hanukkah Bouquet for Peaches Rosen's Hanukkah, and she paid bupkus.

HESTER. *(To* **JESS**.*)* What's your name, girl?

JESS. Jess Wilder.

ANN. Jess, it's a pleasure to meet you.

EDIE. It's a godsend you're here!

HESTER. *(Suspicious.)* Why *are* you here?

ANN. Is this a school project?

JESS. No. School and I kinda broke up.

EDIE. Well, joining the Historical Society is a very educational experience.

HESTER. Have you been in our museum before?

JESS. Once. In third grade. The other years I had the flu.

HESTER.	**EDIE.**	**ANN.**
Right.	Uh-huh.	Really.

EDIE. Jess, would you like us to show you around?

HESTER. I'm not done with my battle plan!

ANN. *(To* **JESS.***)* We're trying to think of ways to boost membership and raise money.

JESS. Awesome.

EDIE. And, see? We have a new member already!

HESTER. Flank two: Poverty. If visitors don't pay to come to the mountain we drop the mountain on top of them. We put a travelling exhibit together and charge admission. We'll build up our treasury and get publicity in every town we visit.

ANN. What do we have that people would pay money to see?

HESTER. Pick any one of our displays!

*(***HESTER** *opens the cover of a wooden box big enough to hold a soccer ball.)*

JESS. *(Peering in.)* What is it?

HESTER. The World's Largest Hairball!

JESS. *(Stepping back, repulsed.)* A hairball? That's totally gross. And I hate cats.

EDIE. Me too. And don't tell me "nine lives" isn't satanic.

HESTER. It's not a cat hairball, it's a pig hairball.

JESS. Pigs hock hairballs?

HESTER. Not only do they, but in 1885 the largest hairball in history was hocked right here in New Bunion by a pig owned by Farmer William Wilde.

EDIE. "Hog" Wilde.

HESTER. Farmer Wilde had the largest collection of hog hairballs in New England. During his funeral service another hairball collector broke in and stole every one of them.

EDIE. They fetched a fortune on the hairball black market.

HESTER. Luckily, Farmer Wilde had already donated this hairball to us, so it's still here for the world to see.

> (**HESTER** *gets out what looks like a lead-coated soccer ball.*)

JESS. *(Takes it, puzzled.)* Where's all the hair? This is metal.

HESTER. In 1936 the Historical Society was worried the ball was losing its hair so to preserve it they dipped it in lead.

EDIE. So, Jess, how much could we charge to hold the hairball?

HESTER. Twenty dollars.

ANN. Three.

JESS. Zero.

HESTER. Fifteen.

ANN. Two fifty.

JESS. Zip.

HESTER. Five dollars!

ANN. Jess, what could you buy for five dollars?

JESS. A latte, maybe two song downloads.

HESTER. You want music? How about this? An original Edison phonograph.

> (*She pulls out an old Edison cylinder phonograph and a rare 1929 recording of the Leo Bunion Orchestra.*)

EDIE. "Harelip" Hicks, went to his death blowing a High "C."

> (*We hear first notes of a march,* then the cylinder recording slows, stops.*)

---

*A license to produce *George Washington's Teeth* does not include a performance license for any third-party or copyrighted music. Licensees should create an original composition or use music in the public domain. For further information, please see Music Use Note on page 3.

ANN. *(To* **JESS.***)* Got your five dollars' worth?

HESTER. Wait! How about this?

> *(She takes out a small object from a case, shriveled, unrecognizable.)*

Here is the first elected mayor of New Bunion, Joshua Dewlap.

JESS. They shrunk his head?

HESTER. No! In the 1870s we were known primarily for our Sunny Blaze apples –

EDIE. Named after our famous pyromaniac, Sunny Blaze.

HESTER. The town decided that rather than honor Mayor Dewlap with a conventional statue they would carve his face into a Sunny Blaze.

EDIE. They even took the actual wart from his chin and glued it on. It's right here – *(Points.)*

JESS. Are you punking me?

ANN. Sadly, no. This is our collection.

HESTER. We haven't scratched the surface! What about our beaver tail tambourine? Or our wingless owl?

JESS. This place is so beat. Except for that thing –

> *(Hester's moose chair.)*

It's, like, *Game of Thrones*.

HESTER. That is *not* a throne.

JESS. The TV *Game of Thrones*?

HESTER. I don't waste my time with game shows. Did you have relatives on the Mayflower?

ANN. Hester!

> *(***EDIE** *intervenes, pointing to a row of colonists' portraits on the wall.)*

EDIE. This is our Wall of Heroes. These Bunionites played important parts in the American Revolution. Captain Ferdie Collier – he was the reason George Washington trusted Benedict Arnold for so long.

ANN. Ferdie believed he could tell a man's character by reading the lines in his palm. He swore there was no way Arnold was a traitor.

EDIE. Washington refused to believe Ferdie was blind as a bat until he saw him buttering his pocket watch.

HESTER. Those are the Gardner brothers –

JESS. *(Indicating the wall.)* Wait. Where are the women?

ANN. Pardon?

JESS. The women who fought in the Revolution.

HESTER. No women "fought" in the Revolution. They stayed home, watched the children, and ran the farm.

JESS. That's not all they did. Look at the three of you, right? You run this place, but is that all you do?

HESTER. I was Principal of Bunion Hill Elementary. I still substitute.

EDIE. Her classes never act up, Hester terrifies them.

HESTER. *(Proudly.)* Like I did their parents before them.

EDIE. I'm the florist downtown. I own Hearts and Flowers.

JESS. The place with the worms in the window?

EDIE. It's my "Underground Garden" display.

JESS. *(To* **ANN.***)* What do you do?

ANN. *(Uncomfortable.)* I guess you could say I'm a domestic manager. I supervise my household and the staff.

EDIE. That's not all she does! Ann's also a trophy wife.

HESTER. Forget what *we* do. What makes *you* the expert on women in the Revolution?

JESS. I'm no expert. I just took Women's Studies. Hold on.

(She takes out her iPhone and speaks into it.)

American Revolution. Women. Heroes.

IPHONE. *(Recording.)* Searching.

EDIE. Aren't these phones amazing? Today, you don't have to think at all.

IPHONE. *(Recording.)* American Revolution. Women. Heroes.

JESS. Check it out! A whole list of women.

(*Reading.*) Rachel and Grace Martin. They disguised themselves as men and fought the whole war.

ANN. I didn't know that.

HESTER. But they fought as "men." Why would that count?

JESS. Okay...

(*Reading.*) Hannah Black, North Carolina. She was a spy. She carried secret messages and hid soldiers at her farm until the British burned it down. Martha Bratton blew up British soldiers' gunpowder. Elizabeth Burgin helped rescue 200 Americans from New York prison ships.

ANN. This is fascinating.

JESS. Why don't you do a Revolutionary Women exhibit? That would be bitchin'.

HESTER. We don't care about "bitchin'." We care about history.

EDIE. We just do a lot of bitchin'.

ANN. Jess, it's a great idea. Do you have any other thoughts about exhibits that would really interest you?

JESS. I'm thinking.

(*Pause.*)

Well, last year I saw something sweet in Black Studies.

HESTER. Why would you take "Black Studies"?

JESS. "Why?"

HESTER. You're not black. That's like a man taking Women Studies.

ANN. Hester, that's ridiculous.

JESS. Did you ever study a language?

HESTER. Of course I did. French.

JESS. Why? Are you French? People should, like, learn about each other, right? Isn't that why there's museums?

EDIE. Can I quote that?

(*To* **HESTER** *and* **ANN**.) I want to put out a press release announcing our twenty-five percent increase in membership.

ANN. Jess, what were you saying you saw in class?

JESS. Oh. We saw George Washington's teeth.

ANN. *President* George Washington's teeth?

JESS. Oh yeah. My father was so pissed he missed it. He's an orthodontist.

ANN. I thought Washington had wooden teeth.

JESS. Myth. But his teeth were terrible. Rotting, falling out. He had new dentures made all the time; it was a major pain in the ass.

He had one pair made here, in New Bunion. That's why he stayed two days.

HESTER. Three.

ANN. Two.

HESTER. I've never heard about these teeth. Someone's pulling a fast one on you.

JESS. No way. My professor asked the woman who owns them to come in and show us.

ANN. Who's that?

JESS. *(Thinks.)* Louisa Tye. She lives here. Unless she moved, or died. She was, like, your age.

HESTER. There's no Taiwanese woman in New Bunion.

ANN. "Tye" is her last name.

HESTER. Either way, I don't believe it. If anyone in town had George Washington's teeth I would know about it.

JESS. Chill. I'll check it out.

(Takes out iPhone, talks into it.) Call Louisa Tye, New Bunion.

IPHONE. *(Recording, friendly voice.)* Dialing Louisa Tye.

EDIE. Your phone seems nice. Mine is so judgmental.

HESTER. She better not be dead.

(They listen to one ring after another.)

JESS. *(Gets an answer.)* Hey, Mrs. Tye? This is Jess Wilder, I heard you talk at Professor Bader's Black History class last spring... Yeah, you were awesome. I was just telling some people about you and George Washington's teeth... Right... Is there any way I can bring them over to see them? ...Oh. Got it.

HESTER. What?

JESS. She just packed up her whole collection. She's donating everything to the Smithsonian.

EDIE. No!

ANN. Ask if we could just talk with her.

JESS. Mrs. Tye... You heard that.

(Listens.) She's leaving town tomorrow. She doesn't have time to see anyone.

(To Louisa.) No problem, Mrs. Tye, I just thought it would be cool if you and these museum people met.

...The New Bunion Museum... Yeah, I'm here... Really? Hold on.

(Surprised.) She could see you guys for a few minutes tomorrow morning. Does that work?

(The women agree.)

HESTER. Tell her to come here. 631 Hamilton Turnpike. Turn right at Harvey's Barbershop.

EDIE. *(To* **ANN.***)* Harvey just cut off three fingers in a shaving accident. We sent him Pick Me Up Posies but he couldn't pick them up.

JESS. How about ten o'clock tomorrow? ...Okay, awesome... See you then.

(Hangs up.)

Done deal. She seems really excited to meet you.

HESTER. Of course she is.

EDIE. This can be our salvation.

ANN. If she would just loan us the teeth for a few months we'll have visitors lining up.

EDIE. This would be like having Kennedy's back brace, or Taft's kidney stones.

ANN. There must be other museums that have Washington's dentures.

HESTER. That doesn't matter! These are Washington's New Bunion Teeth!

EDIE. *(Thrilled, moved.)* We're saved! We need help, she walks in… I… Oh boy.

> (**EDIE** *starts to swoon;* **HESTER** *and* **ANN** *sit her down.*)

ANN.	**HESTER.**
Easy.	Sit down, girl!
Good!	There you go.

JESS. Is she okay?

ANN. She's fine. It happens any time she's stressed.

HESTER. She stresses at yellow lights.

ANN. Jess, we can't thank you enough.

JESS. No worries. *(Takes out a paper.)* Can somebody sign this, though? And say, like, I was here for three hours? Or make it ten, for finding the teeth, okay?

ANN. *(Takes paper and reads.)* Community service?

JESS. It's part of my probation. See you tomorrow.

HESTER. Did you say "probation"?

JESS. Yeah. It counts toward "time served."

ANN. Jail time served?

JESS. Wow, I could tell you stories.

> (**EDIE** *stirs.*)

But not with her around. Later.

> (**JESS** *exits.* **EDIE** *opens her eyes.*)

EDIE. What did I miss?

HESTER. A serial killer.

> *(Lights go down.* **RADIO ANNOUNCER** *is heard, fife and bugle music behind him.*)*

---

*A license to produce *George Washington's Teeth* does not include a performance license for any third-party or copyrighted music. Licensees should create an original composition or use music in the public domain. For further information, please see Music Use Note on page 3.

ANNOUNCER. *(Voice-over.)* It's that time again: the American Revolution Reenactment on the grounds of the New Bunion Historical Society this Saturday, the Fourth of July! Free snuff and Johnnycakes. And bring the kids! The reenactors promise twice the blood they spilled last year! And as they say, "The Battle of New Bunion never happened, but if it did, ours is still bigger."

> *(The next morning. Lights up on the museum.* **JESS** *strolls around looking at exhibits.* **ANN** *enters, keys in her hand.)*

JESS. Hey.

ANN. Hi. I thought we locked the door last night.

JESS. You did.

ANN. Then how did you get in?

JESS. I had my pen knife and library card.

ANN. I don't get it.

> *(***JESS*** takes both out of her pocket.)*

JESS. It's simple. You cut a "V" in the end of any hard plastic card, right? Then you slide it between the door and the doorjamb, fit the "V" around the latch, and pull down. You need better security.

ANN. I'll bring that up.

(Hesitant.) Did you learn that…in prison?

JESS. Nah. *McGruff the Crime Dog*. Hey, I didn't mean to put you on the spot yesterday. You know, when I asked what you do and you said basically nothing. Everybody has their own thing, right?

ANN. Sure. But I didn't mean I did "nothing." I do a lot of charity work besides helping out here. And I represent the Mather Trust at a lot of functions.

JESS. "Functions" meaning…parties?

ANN. Well, business parties.

JESS. You have kids?

ANN. No. My husband has two and that's enough abuse. I go to the gym every day, keep our social calendar,

and I'm responsible for everything about the property. Hiring staff, maintenance. It's a *big* house.
(Realizing who she's talking with.) With a great security system.

JESS. What do you have?

ANN. Safe Well.

JESS. Change to Storm Front.

ANN. Thanks. And I should mention that before I got married I had a career in art restoration.

JESS. That sounds awesome. You must need a lot of training.

ANN. You start with school, then there's apprenticeships and certification. The restoration work was fascinating, but I mostly loved being around the art every day. This museum is the closest thing I have to it.

JESS. I don't really get art. What's good or what's bad. I could stand there all day and stare at a squiggle on a black canvas and not figure out if it's worth two dollars or two million.

ANN. You can't look at it that way. The value is only what it's worth for you. And restoring artwork is like bringing it back to life. It's like being there when it was first created.

JESS. If you loved it so much, why did you stop working?

ANN. Life.
(Trying for lightness.) You'd be amazed how not working takes so much time.

JESS. I know it's, like, really cheesy to talk about money. But sometimes you have to throw one of those grenade questions since it's gonna blow sooner or later.

ANN. Go on and toss it.

JESS. You guys must have shitloads of cash.

ANN. Yeah. Shitloads.

(HESTER enters with EDIE.)

HESTER. Where's the Taiwanese woman?

JESS. She's not Taiwanese. Her name is "Tye."

HESTER. Either way, she should be early. Remember that, girl. My grandmother taught me that for every minute we're late we'll burn in hell.

JESS. I'm here already.

EDIE. Hi, Jess, are you excited? I am so excited!

ANN. Don't get your hopes up, or your blood pressure.

(Sound of car approaching and parking.)

JESS. *(Looking out.)* That's her.
  (To **HESTER.***)* On time. I'll get her.

  *(***JESS** *exits.)*

ANN. *(Lowering her voice.)* Did you find out anything about her criminal record?

EDIE. Her records are sealed. AND we've never delivered a single flower to her.

HESTER. *Nobody* sends flowers to Death Row.

  *(***JESS** *enters with* **LOUISA TYE,** *who looks around the museum, unimpressed.* **JESS** *is carrying a metal case with a lock on it.)*

JESS. Guys, this is Mrs. Tye.

ANN. Mrs. Tye, thanks for making the time to see us.

LOUISA. Please call me "Louisa."

ANN. "Ann."

EDIE. *(Puts her hand up.)* "Edie"!

HESTER. "Miss Bunion." Let's not get ahead of ourselves.

ANN. Louisa, have you been in our museum before?

LOUISA. Once. I believe I was in second grade. Other years I had the flu.

HESTER.	**ANN.**	**EDIE.**	**JESS.**
Right.	Did you?	You too?	Oh yeah.

HESTER. *(Indicates metal box.)* Are the teeth in there?

LOUISA. Let's not get ahead of ourselves. I believe Jessica told you that I've donated my collection to the Smithsonian except for the pieces on tour.

ANN. "On tour"?

LOUISA. Yes. My exhibit travelling to museums as a benefit for the African American Heritage Society. It's been very popular – we've met our fundraising goals already.

HESTER. Well, isn't that peachy.

ANN. Did we hear you're leaving town?

LOUISA. Yes. I'll be spending a year as a guest curator in Liverpool.

EDIE. *(Excited.)* A Beatles museum?

LOUISA. No. The National Museum of Slavery.

> (**LOUISA** *unlocks the long metal box.*)

I thought you might like to see some pieces from my collection. These are the most fragile objects. I was afraid to send them with the movers so I'm driving them to Washington myself. I'd appreciate it if you look but don't touch.

> *(Hands the small, clear glass container to* **JESS**, *who inspects it.)*

EDIE. It's like church, but exciting!

JESS. What is this?

LOUISA. Strands of John Quincy Adams' hair.

HESTER. He was nearly bald. How do you know it's really his?

LOUISA. John Quincy's great-great-grandson has a lock of it. He traded those strands for my knee breech buckle worn by the Marquis de Lafayette.

> *(She grabs a small box, opens it.)*

This is a miniature ivory portrait of Thomas Jefferson. It was painted in Philadelphia by Charles Willson Peale, who was the most famous miniature artist of his time. It was covered in sediment but I had the most famous restorer of *our* time save it.

ANN. *(Looks closer.)* Interesting.

> (**ANN** *reaches for it.*)

LOUISA. No touching!

(She takes out a small, beautifully carved box and unlocks it.)

And here, ladies, are the teeth of the Father of our Country.

HESTER. *(Awed.)* George Washington's teeth.

JESS. Neato.

ANN. *(Awed.)* I just got a chill.

EDIE. Does anybody think they look a little...large?

HESTER. A big man has a big mouth. He was six foot one.

LOUISA. Actually, he stood six foot two.

HESTER. One.

LOUISA. Two.

HESTER. What's his shoe size?

LOUISA. Thirteen. Weight?

HESTER. He went from 175 to 200. Favorite food?

LOUISA. Cream of peanut soup.

HESTER. Middle name?

LOUISA. He had none.

*(**HESTER** thought she had her on that one.)*

His dogs' names?

HESTER. Tartar...True Love...and Sweet Kiss.

LOUISA. Sweet Lips.

HESTER. Kiss.

LOUISA. Lips.

ANN. *(Cutting them off.)* What college did George Washington go to?

LOUISA & HESTER. HE DIDN'T.

EDIE. That's where I went.

JESS. So if Washington's teeth weren't made of wood, what were they?

LOUISA. That's the myth. They were made with all sorts of things – lead, cow teeth, ivory, even hippopotamus bone.

JESS. Woah.

HESTER. How'd you get these?

LOUISA. Why don't we all sit down?

>*(They do.)*

My family came to New Bunion in 1741.

HESTER. A little late to the party.

ANN. Hester!

HESTER. Mine came in '39!

JESS. *(To* **EDIE.***)* This is better than a cage fight.

ANN. New Bunion's settlement couldn't be more than a hundred people, then. Your families must have known each other.

LOUISA. I have no doubt about that. There have always been Tyes here since.

My grandson Edgar is one of the reenactors this weekend for that yearly sham battle.

HESTER. How'd you get the teeth?

LOUISA. My ancestor, James Tye, was a blacksmith; the only one in these parts. That made him an important man. He didn't just make hardware and horseshoes; he made hatchets, knives, bullets – and he couldn't make enough of them. Especially once the war started.

HESTER. Patriot or Tory?

LOUISA. Patriot, of course. And dentist.

EDIE. Dentist?

LOUISA. At that time, blacksmiths did more than metal work. If someone needed a tooth pulled or dentures made, they called a blacksmith.

JESS. Washington.

LOUISA. *(Nods.)* As his teeth kept falling out he needed more and more replacements. By the time he was inaugurated he had only one real tooth left.

Washington saved his teeth that fell out, but most were useless, so he had to find others and get a new set made. James Tye made them. He saved the ivory teeth that hadn't cracked but Washington needed nine new ones.

JESS. What did he use for the teeth?

LOUISA. They were human teeth. Washington bought them right here in New Bunion.

ANN. From who?

LOUISA. Slaves.

EDIE. I didn't know we had slaves in New Bunion.

HESTER. Because we didn't.

LOUISA. You're wrong.

JESS. *(To* **HESTER.***)* Time for a Black History course, Hester.

HESTER. New Bunion was founded by Quakers! Quakers were always opposed to slavery!

LOUISA. They were the first colonists to protest it back in 1688, but the majority of Quakers ignored them. It wasn't till 1774 that it became Quaker Doctrine. And George Washington passed through New Bunion in –

ANN. 1773.

HESTER. How do you know Washington bought these teeth from *our* slaves?

LOUISA. His journals. You can read them at Mount Vernon. He kept detailed records on everything he bought. Nine teeth for 122 shillings. That's less than the going rate, but slaves' teeth were a bargain. President Washington was very happy with James' work and gave him his old set. Now, before I go, there are a few special objects I'd like to show you. Jess, can you give me a hand?

JESS. You got it.

*(***LOUISA** *and* **JESS** *leave.)*

EDIE. *(Stricken.)* We're doomed!

HESTER. Dial it back, girl.

ANN. *(Lowering her voice.)* She won't loan us Washington's teeth, but we can ask to borrow some other pieces from her collection.

*(***HESTER** *opens the box containing the teeth.)*

ANN. What are you doing?

HESTER. I don't believe a word that woman says. I want a closer look.

ANN. Don't you dare!

EDIE. They're fragile!

ANN. Hester, they'll break!

HESTER. Don't be Nervous Nellies, I'm just taking a look.

> (**HESTER** *has the teeth out and holds them up to look closer.*)

EDIE. Please, please, please.

ANN. Put them back!

HESTER. I will, I will...

ANN. *(Crosses to* **HESTER.***)* Do it now!

> (**ANN** *grabs* **HESTER***'s hands.* **HESTER** *pulls back, and the teeth fly up and over her head.* **EDIE** *catches them with both hands.*)

EDIE. Somebody take them! They're chattering!

HESTER. That's you!

ANN. Don't move!

HESTER. *(Looks out the door.)* They're coming!

> (*Like a hot potato,* **EDIE** *lobs the teeth to* **HESTER***, who tosses them to* **ANN***.*)

> (*As* **LOUISA** *and* **JESS** *enter carrying display boxes,* **ANN** *puts the teeth between her knees – and moves behind the moose chair.*)

LOUISA. And here we are.

HESTER. Here they are!

EDIE. They're back!

ANN. Look who's here!

LOUISA. *(Suspicious.)* If everyone could gather round.

JESS. Ann! Check it out.

> (*As the others stare at the objects instead of her,* **ANN** *wobbles toward them, the teeth held between her knees.*)

LOUISA. These were some of the artifacts we uncovered on Tye property when we laid the foundation for the restored barn.

> (**ANN** *surreptitiously takes the teeth.* **HESTER** *opens the box, puts them in, and slams the box closed.*)
>
> (**LOUISA**, *hearing the box, turns to them, puzzled.*)
>
> (**EDIE** *speaks loudly to distract* **LOUISA**.)

EDIE. A TEA SPOON?

LOUISA. Yes.

EDIE. Amazing!

ANN. Is that a bell?

LOUISA. It is.

JESS. Like, a dinner bell?

LOUISA. Actually, it was attached to a slave collar so the slave owner could hear where he or she was. It was used as punishment, especially for runaways.

HESTER. What are those?

LOUISA. They're children's shackles. The child must have been five or six.

> (*All look, horrified.*)

Because they were found here it makes sense that my ancestor, James Tye, made all of these. And I'm sure his own.

JESS. So, James was –

LOUISA. A slave, yes. If you have any interest, I can show you some other metalwork we unearthed.

JESS. Do it!

ANN. Louisa, we're very, very interested. We'd also love if you could see to loaning us any pieces from your collection to the museum.

LOUISA. I'm afraid that's impossible. I have plans for all of it.

JESS. Bummer.

ANN. They would only be on loan for as long as you like.

EDIE. Or as short as you like.

HESTER. They can go other places afterwards, can't they?

LOUISA. *(Undecided.)* I'm usually very familiar with a museum's reputation before I work with them. What do you normally do to commemorate Black History Month?

(**HESTER, ANN,** *and* **EDIE** *look at her blankly.*)

JESS. Oh no...

ANN. *(Lost.)* How do we *normally* commemorate it? Hester?

HESTER. Normally??

ANN. Normally.

HESTER. We usually wing it.

EDIE. It depends on what month it falls on.

LOUISA. It always falls on the same month. When do *you* recognize it?

ANN. This year?

HESTER. Yes.

ANN. March.

EDIE. May.

HESTER. *(Loudest.)* October.

LOUISA. *(To* **HESTER.***)* It's in February.

ANN. Louisa, I'll be honest. We've never celebrated Black History Month.

LOUISA. Or Kwanzaa, I imagine.

EDIE. We don't even know him.

ANN. I promise, with your help, we'll celebrate Black History Month this February. Please give us the chance.

LOUISA. I don't know. When I lend anything from my collection I have strict protocols that need to be followed. They must be used in children's education, for example. I like to get the community involved, especially the artists. Tie the history to storytelling, music, and dance.

EDIE. We can do that! Can't we do that?

HESTER. Easy, Edie.

ANN. It's a terrific idea.

LOUISA. *(Unsure.)* It means a lot of work. There's a dance group in Boston that I like to work with. It specializes in recreating early African American song and dance. Have you ever seen them?

EDIE. Have any of them been on *Dancing With the Stars*?

HESTER. Shush!

LOUISA. Do you have something to play music?

JESS. Oh yeah.

> *(**JESS** gets out her phone.)*

iTunes? YouTube? Google Play?

LOUISA. Google "Ring Shout, 'Wade in the Water.'" The Ring Shout is a dance that was done by slaves and there's every chance it was done here in New Bunion. "Wade in the Water" was written before the Civil War. It was one of Harriet Tubman's favorite hymns. I won't ask if you knew who she was.

ANN. Wasn't she a slave?

LOUISA. She was. She rescued others through the Underground Railroad.

*(To **EDIE**.)* It was not a real railroad. It was a group of people who helped slaves escape north into free states. They put their lives on the line, like Harriet did. Now the Ring Shout started with slaves as a religious experience. People moved in a circle, clapping and shouting out when the Spirit moved them.

> *(**LOUISA** nods at **JESS**, who turns on the music.)*
>
> *(**LOUISA** demonstrates the clapping and movement, later singing with the recording.)*

JESS. *(Trying it.)* Is this right?

LOUISA. There you go!

JESS. Ann! Come in!

EDIE. Me too!

*(Passes **HESTER**.)*

Come on, Hester!

LOUISA.
> SEE THAT BAND ALL DRESSED IN WHITE
> GOD'S GONNA TROUBLE THE WATER
> IT LOOKS LIKE A BAND OF ISRAELITES
> GOD'S GONNA TROUBLE THE WATER.

*(**JESS** grabs the beaver drum.)*

LOUISA, ANN & EDIE.
> WADE IN THE WATER
> WADE IN THE WATER, CHILDREN,
> WADE IN THE WATER,
> GOD'S GONNA TROUBLE THE WATER.

*(Music stops. **LOUISA**, **ANN**, and **EDIE** sing chorus again, a capella.)*

> WADE IN THE WATER
> WADE IN THE WATER, CHILDREN,
> WADE IN THE WATER,
> GOD'S GONNA TROUBLE THE WATER.

EDIE. Oh boy...

*(**ANN** realizes what is coming, stops singing. **LOUISA** continues shaking her staff and singing, **JESS** continues drumming.)*

JESS. Woo!

ANN. We should stop...

LOUISA. Wait!

*(It's as if the spirit has taken over **EDIE**. She emits her usual sound, now higher. Hands and eyes raised to Heaven, dancing in her own circle.)*

EDIE. AMEN! HOSANNA!

ANN. Edie...

EDIE. PASS THE BASKET!

ANN. JESS! STOP!

(**JESS** *does.* **EDIE** *snaps out of it.*)

EDIE. What did I miss?

LOUISA. Not one beat.

JESS. You guys are better than drugs.

ANN. *(To* **LOUISA**.*)* We'd love to have dance as part of our exhibition.

HESTER. We're not a church choir, we're a historical organization! Why would anyone want to hear a Sunday school song about splashing in the water? What's educational about that?

LOUISA. It's not just a "Sunday school song," Hester. The lyrics are slave code. "Wade in the Water" means that when the slave owners' dogs are chasing you, get off the land and into a stream or river – dogs can't follow your scent there.

JESS. Good move...

LOUISA. The "woman dressed in white" is Tubman, helping slaves find freedom. Slave songs were more than songs, they had secret meanings.

ANN. I had no idea.

LOUISA. Things are not always what they seem.

ANN. We'd love to have your input for the exhibition.

HESTER. Not so fast! We have exhibit policies as well, Mrs. Tye. Especially for "outsiders." We need to have a notarized statement of authenticity and ultimate control of how the exhibit is curated.

EDIE. We do?

HESTER. Absolutely. We don't want anyone making statements about what you claim to be "Slave History" that we don't endorse.

JESS. You want to "endorse" slavery?

HESTER. Of course not! I want to exhibit history at this museum, not folk tales. So tell us, Mrs. Tye, do you want to work with us or not?

LOUISA. It's so funny you say that. My grandmother actually visited this museum years ago.

ANN. When?

LOUISA. I think it was in the fall of 1954. My family always told a story about that.

JESS. What is it?

LOUISA. Grandmother brought in some of her artifacts to show the Historical Society. Some of the same ones I've shown you today, actually.

ANN. Really!

HESTER. *My* grandmother was president in '54.

LOUISA. Yes, she was. Your grandmother was the person who threw my grandmother out.

EDIE. What?

HESTER. That couldn't have happened.

LOUISA. That's just what she told my grandmother.

JESS. Why? They should have gone nuts on this stuff!

LOUISA. You would think so.

(*To* **HESTER**.) But she had the exact same reaction you did. She refused to believe her Quaker ancestors owned slaves, even when my grandmother showed her the Tye Family Bible. All our lineage is written in the back of it. Actually, I doubt she ever finished reading it. She stopped when she saw the name Sampson Bunion.

HESTER. My Sampson?

LOUISA. Sampson Bunion was the biggest slaveholder in this county.

ANN. *What?*

JESS. My head just exploded.

HESTER. That can't be right! This is slanderous! No Bunion, especially Sampson, would have owned slaves!

LOUISA. But he did. And I should know. My family was his "property."

ANN. I'm confused. Is that why his name's in your family Bible?

LOUISA. No. He's in our Bible because he had a child with one of his slaves. Her name was Louisa.

HESTER. *Louisa?*

LOUISA. The first Louisa. I was named after her.

HESTER. No! That's impossible!

LOUISA. I will swear to it on the Tye Family Bible.

ANN. *(Realizing.)* So that makes Hester…

LOUISA. Exactly.

(Turns to **HESTER.***)* Hester and I are great, great, great, great, great half-sisters.

*(***HESTER** *is frozen in shock.)*

EDIE. That's Great!

*(***HESTER** *passes out and hits the floor.)*

LOUISA. *(Pause.)* Let's help up Sister Hester.

(The Edison phonograph bursts to life playing something like "Happy Days are Here Again."*)

(Blackout.)

(Music morphs into a current recording of the New Bunyon marching band.** The event **ANNOUNCER** *is heard.)*

ANNOUNCER. *(Voice-over.)* Those sweet sounds come from the New Bunion Volunteer Marching Band. We want to give Harvey Beard a big shout-out for playing piccolo with just two fingers.

---

*A license to produce *George Washington's Teeth* does not include a performance license for "Happy Days are Here Again." The publisher and author suggest that the licensee contact ASCAP or BMI to ascertain the music publisher and contact such music publisher to license or acquire permission for performance of the song. If a license or permission is unattainable for "Happy Days are Here Again," the licensee may not use the song in *George Washington's Teeth* but should create an original composition in a similar style or use a similar song in the public domain. For further information, please see Music Use Note on page 3.

**A license to produce *George Washington's Teeth* does not include a performance license for any third-party or copyrighted music. Licensees should create an original composition or use music in the public domain. For further information, please see Music Use Note on page 3.

This is WNBN on the grounds of the New Bunion Historical Society and the British are coming! Actually, they're already here and setting up camp. But unless our colonists are hidden behind the trees, we haven't caught sight of them yet. Don't touch that dial! We'll be right back with the Battle of New Bunion.

(Lights up on the museum. **EDIE**, **HESTER**, *and* **ANN** *are working.* **EDIE** *arranging flowers,* **ANN** *polishing the moose chair,* **HESTER** *dusting.)*

ANN. There's one thing they never teach us about history.

EDIE. What's that?

ANN. It always bites you in the ass.

HESTER. I've seen no proof of "history" in anything that woman said.

ANN. Hester, stop. It's *your* family that's been hiding your heritage.

EDIE. And Louisa's right. We haven't had one Black History exhibit ever.

HESTER. *(Arguing.)* Because they're not interested! How many Black children came to the museum this year for New Bunion Day?

EDIE. John Redwood, Tanya Curry, Earl Tait, Mary Green...

HESTER. Go pass out, Edie.

(To **ANN.***)* Have you talked to Jayden about his foundation's donation yet?

ANN. *(Steeling herself.)* Yes, I did.

EDIE. Thank the Lord! How much will Jayden give us this year?

ANN. Nothing.

HESTER. Nothing?

ANN. I'm sorry, but there's no donation. He... Well... I haven't told you, but technically we're not a couple at the moment.

EDIE. Because you're not staying together in the city?

ANN. Because he's staying there with Angela, his trophy wife in training. I was so naïve. No, stupid. I wouldn't let myself believe that a man who left his first wife for a younger woman would do it again. I guess I thought I'd be enough, or at least I'd wear him out. He's living with his yoga instructor. I gave him that class as a Christmas present – I thought it would help him relax.

HESTER. Doubt he's doing much of that.

ANN. She's twenty-two; he's almost triple that. I really can't talk about this.

EDIE. Look on the bright side: you also might be giving him a heart attack.

HESTER. Well, then, our cookie is crumbled. We can't go one more month with an empty bank account.

EDIE. There's still that grant from the cultural council.

HESTER. I'll go get the mail.

> (**HESTER** *opens the door and walks out. We hear the band before she closes the door behind her.*)

EDIE. Ann, I am so sorry.

ANN. I appreciate that.

EDIE. Do you have a prenup?

ANN. Of course. It's ironclad, except in a case of adultery.

EDIE. But Jayden committed adultery.

ANN. Not until after he filed for a legal separation. On Valentine's Day.

EDIE. You know, Ann, you have to keep positive. When my mother died, I didn't know what I'd do. In the market, every time I saw "soup for one" I'd start sobbing. The trick is to keep yourself busy. I keep the shop open now on Sundays and an hour later every day. By the time I get home I'm so tired all I want is take-out and *Jeopardy*. When a holiday's coming, you go on the offensive. Christmas is the worst. Do what I do: send yourself Christmas cards. Lots of them. The mailman and anyone who stops by will think you have a great social life. And you know what else? I sign the cards from famous people. This year I got cards from Betty White, Joe Biden, and the Bachelor. I got one from the White House, too, but I refused delivery.

ANN. Edie, can I throw you a grenade question?

EDIE. Sure. Sometimes you've just got to chuck one out there.

ANN. Why don't you invite Humphrey Hodkins out to dinner or a movie one night?

EDIE. How can you even say that? We're arch-enemies!

ANN. No, I think you've been crazy about him since grammar school, when he threw you in the dumpster. Boys only throw girls they like in the dumpster.

EDIE. I don't know about that.

ANN. I do. I shot Brad Clark in back of his head with paper clips for years. And he'd trip me every time I walked by his desk. The day I passed him without hitting the floor I thought, "It's over." The only person even shyer than you in this town is Humphrey Hodkins. Just ask him. He'll say "yes" or "no." Think about it.

EDIE. I do. A lot.

*(**HESTER** enters with a pile of mail, waving a large brown envelope.)*

HESTER. We heard back from the cultural council!

ANN. This fast?

EDIE. Open it!

*(**HESTER** tears the envelope open.)*

ANN. That's our grant application, isn't it?

HESTER. I don't understand. This is the cover letter I wrote them.

*(**EDIE** has picked up the envelope and reads it.)*

EDIE. 631 Hamilton Turnpike. That's us.

HESTER. That's the return address.

ANN. It is. But it's also the address you sent the grant to.

HESTER. It can't be.
(Takes the envelope and reads it.) 631... Oh no. Oh no.

EDIE. What happened?

ANN. She mailed it to herself.

HESTER. We're finished. I killed us.

EDIE. *(As much to herself as to them.)* Stay calm! Don't panic! Let's just put our heads together.

ANN. That's probably the worst thing we could do.

(JESS enters. Noise outside is heard.)

ANNOUNCER. *(Voice-over.)* Still no sign of the colonists! We have got ourselves some very cranky Brits...

JESS. *(Upbeat.)* Hey, people.

ANN. Hey.

EDIE. Hi, Jess.

JESS. Listen, I was wondering. Could you put down that this week I worked, like, forty hours?

HESTER. "Like forty hours"? It's not "*like*" forty hours! It's either "forty hours" or it's not! And for what? Introducing us to that useless Tye woman?

JESS. No. For this.

(She takes George Washington's teeth from her pocket and puts them down before the women.)

HESTER. Are those...

JESS. Ohhh yeah.

HESTER. You stole George Washington's teeth?

JESS. *Borrowed* his teeth.

ANN. Why would you do that?

JESS. I've got this problem. My shrink says I have an "impulse control disorder" and my lawyer says I'm "incorrigible." The prosecutor said he doesn't care which as long as I'm off the streets.

ANN. Is that why you went to prison?

JESS. I got busted for taking some stuff from a restaurant.

HESTER. They locked you up for that?

EVA. I sometimes sneak an extra "Sweet and Lows."

HESTER. What are we talking about here? Salt shakers, cutlery?

JESS. A cappuccino machine, three bottles of wine, and a Ferrari in the parking lot.

ANN. Jess, why would you take these teeth? You know Louisa's going to call the police the minute she sees the box is empty.

JESS. But it's not. Remember I said my dad's an orthodontist? He was so bummed he didn't see George Washington's teeth he made his own; he checked out all the pictures he could find. He wanted the teeth for his collection. He's already made copies of Queen Victoria's overbite and Bela Lugosi's partial plate.

HESTER. Louisa can tell a replica from the real thing! And if she can't, the Smithsonian will!

JESS. Sooner or later. But by then she'll be in Liverpool, you'll have your big exhibit and make a fortune with admissions.

ANN. Before they lock us up!

JESS. Here's the thing: You just tell the police I lied and told you Louisa changed her mind and loaned them before she left. The police will check my record, buy it, and I'll be way gone by then.

EVIE. Gone where?

JESS. I'm not sure. Barcelona's famous for its pickpockets, Boston leads with bank robberies. There's a big world out there.

ANN. Well, *we* are not breaking the law. We're returning the teeth.

JESS. Why?

ANN. Because they're stolen!

JESS. Only if you kept them! They'll get their teeth back and you get to keep your museum.

HESTER. It can work.

ANN. No! Edie, you're not going along with this, are you?

EDIE. Well... *(Taking her own pulse.)* I'm not fainting, I'm not hyperventilating.

HESTER. So?

EDIE. My heart's not pounding, I'm not panicking: I say "do it."

JESS. Done. So if one of you guys signs off on my community service so my parole officer's happy I'm out of here.

ANN. Not so fast. What else is in your pockets?

> *(**JESS** starts pulling out objects from her pockets, more than we think possible.)*

EDIE. Mayor Dewlap?

HESTER. Dump the backpack.

ANN. Our beaver tail tambourine!

> *(**JESS** pulls out the hairball.)*

HESTER. How could you fit our hairball in there?

JESS. I'm a professional.

ANN. Jess, why do you do this?

JESS. I'm not sure. When I was a kid I tried to be a magician, but the only trick I loved was making stuff disappear.

HESTER. I don't care if she took half our collection! She's saved our society! That's a happy ending in my book.

> *(**LOUISA**, *furious, barrels through the front door, holding the fake teeth. Band music heard for a moment.*)*

LOUISA. *Where are my teeth?*

> *(She slams the door. All stand shoulder to shoulder to block **LOUISA**'s view of the teeth behind them.)*

EDIE. In your hand.

LOUISA. No! These are false teeth!

JESS. You told us that.

LOUISA. False teeth of the *real* false teeth!

HESTER. But you said some of the false teeth *were* false teeth?

LOUISA. The old false teeth *have* false teeth *and* real teeth to make new false teeth! I can tell a counterfeit when I see it! Do you know how?

EDIE. I'll bite.

> (**LOUISA** *moves around the room, looking. As she's about to pass them and see the teeth, they pivot, still in a straight line, and* **HESTER**, *at the end of the line, reaches back and grabs the teeth.*)

LOUISA. The real false teeth have a kernel of ossified corn stuck between the second and third molars!

HESTER. *(Critical.)* You really should brush more.

> (*As* **LOUISA** *steps closer to* **HESTER**, **HESTER** *passes the teeth behind her back to* **ANN**, *who passes them down to* **JESS**.)

ANN. Maybe the corn just fell out.

> (*The women stand shoulder to shoulder, moving together as* **LOUISA** *tries to look behind them.*)

LOUISA. Not a chance! I would have noticed long ago. And no one touches his teeth but me! Who are you people? The Rockettes?

> (*The women quickly step apart from each other as* **EDIE** *is passed the teeth. She angles so* **LOUISA** *can't see them. She's now the only one with her hands behind her back. She stands stiffly, as if a soldier at attention.*)

What are you doing?

EDIE. Me?

HESTER. She has a nervous personality.

EDIE. I do. I wake up petrified.

ANN. *(Ready to give the teeth up.)* Louisa, I think we can help you.

*(The second **LOUISA** turns to **ANN**, **EDIE** panics – how can she hide the teeth?)*

LOUISA. I don't want your help, I want my teeth!

HESTER. I told you, we don't have them!

LOUISA. The hell you don't! You all look guilty!

*(Turns and points to **EDIE**.)*

Especially you!

*(Terrified, **EDIE** hides the teeth in the only place she can think of – her mouth.)*

ANN. Please don't yell at her.

HESTER. You do, you pick her up!

LOUISA. *(Turns to **EDIE**.)* You expect me to feel sorry for you?

*(**EDIE** turns to face **LOUISA**. Her cheeks are puffed out and she can't say a word. She shrugs as if indifferent and raises her palms up as if she doesn't care.)*

What's wrong with your face?

*(**EDIE** shakes her head, wide-eyed, palms up as if she doesn't understand.)*

ANN. She's having work done.

LOUISA. Did she swallow the work crew?

*(A cell phone rings. Everyone goes for their phone. **JESS** pulls three out of her pocket. It's **LOUISA**'s call.)*

(Answering.) Hello? Edgar! Where are you? ...I'm at your "battleground" right now and the whole town is waiting for you...

You've got to be kidding me! For how long? ...What's wrong with you people? ...Well get off the phone and fix it!

JESS. Your grandson okay?

LOUISA. He and his colonists had a warm-up skirmish with Alamo reenactors outside of Boston. Driving back, their bus broke down. He doesn't know when they'll get here. I'm telling the organizers right now and then I'm going to the police!

ANNOUNCER. *(Voice-over.)* King George III has asked me to make this announcement: if the colonists are not here in the next ten minutes they will consider it as forfeiting the battle. I repeat. Unless our patriots arrive post-haste the British army will declare victory.

HESTER. Dirty Crumpet Munchers.

ANN. Who?

HESTER. The Brits!

LOUISA. They're not British!

HESTER. This can change New Bunion history!

LOUISA. It never was history! Let's stop this nonsense right now!

> *(She sees the bear has a double set of teeth and goes closer to see. **HESTER** blocks her.)*

HESTER. Hold on, girl. We still have ten minutes!

> *(**ANN** grabs the teeth, tossing them to **EDIE**, who puts them back in her mouth.)*

LOUISA. Who is "we"?

HESTER. Us. The colonists.

LOUISA. I'm not a colonist.

HESTER. You're a redcoat?

LOUISA. No!

JESS. So what are you?

LOUISA. The only sane person in this room!

> *(**EDIE** speaks, but her mouth is stretched out by the teeth. We don't understand a word.)*

EDIE. Ffdklsagkdkjgkjdajg.

HESTER. She's right! Today every one of us is either a patriot or a traitor.

ANN. Hester, does it matter? There's nothing we can do even if we wanted to!

HESTER. How many colonial costumes do we have in the storeroom?

ANN. Costumes? I don't know.

HESTER. Edie! Go count them!

> (**EDIE** *rushes into the storeroom, speaking gibberish.*)

Somebody has to teach those lobsterbacks!

LOUISA. You have lost your mind!

ANN. You *have* lost your mind!

HESTER. We've seen this reenactment every year! We know every maneuver! Let's show this town what we're made of!

JESS. Yeah!

HESTER. It's all about our attack!
(To **JESS.***)* Do you play chess?

JESS. No.

HESTER. Checkers?

JESS. No.

ANN. Whac-A-Mole?

JESS. YES! I'm ready to kick Brit butt!

> (**EDIE** *rushes back in and calls out:*)

EDIE. FAKLJFGDJKLSAJGD!!!

HESTER. Perfect! Everyone suit up!

> (**EDIE** *salutes.*)

JESS. Oh, yeah! Let's kick us some Brit butt!

ANN. This is so wrong!

EDIE. Sfdlkasjfkldjfk!

> (**EDIE** *runs back into the storeroom.*)

ANN. *(Calls after her.)* NO!! Edie!! Betsy Ross is my costume!

> (**ANN** *and* **JESS** *run into the storeroom after* **EDIE.***)*

HESTER. No fighting! We've got enough costumes for all of us.

LOUISA. You're not serious.

HESTER. As a kidney stone.

LOUISA. You want me to put on a make-believe costume and pretend to fight a make-believe battle?

HESTER. We're at war!

LOUISA. THERE WAS NO WAR HERE!

HESTER. Is that what you'll tell your grandson? That we lost the Battle of New Bunion because we were one colonist short?

LOUISA. I'm going to tell him the truth. We do that in my family.

> (**LOUISA** *opens the door; we hear the* **ANNOUNCER**.)

ANNOUNCER. *(Voice-over, worried.)* We're at five minutes and counting.

> (*The* **CROWD** *boos.*)

Where's our militia? What will it mean for the outcome of the American Revolution?

> (*The* **CROWD** *reacts.*)

And you redcoats in the parking lot: the Brits did not play beer pong!

LOUISA. How can I even consider doing this?

HESTER. For James Tye!

> (*From the storage room emerge* **JESS** *as Ben Franklin,* **ANN** *as Betsy Ross, and* **EDIE** *as Abraham Lincoln with stovepipe hat and beard.*)

LOUISA. *Lincoln? He wasn't even born yet!*

EDIE. LKSADOIUKDLSA?

HESTER. No, go change! Now!

> (**EDIE** *runs back into the storeroom.*)

JESS. I'm going out there!

> (**JESS** *runs out, grabbing the musket.*)

HESTER. Flank her!

> (**ANN** *picks up the Betsy Ross flag in the stand.*)

LOUISA. *(To* **ANN.***)* You, too? Don't you have any self-respect?

ANN. At this moment in my life? Absolutely none.

> (**ANN** *runs out the door.*)

HESTER. *(Turns to* **LOUISA.***)* Girl, let's tip some Tea Spankers!

LOUISA. "Wankers"! You mean Tea Wankers!

> (**HESTER** *and* **LOUISA** *run into the storeroom.*)

ANNOUNCER. *(Voice-over.)* Ladies and Gentlemen, time is running out! The course of American history is about to change.

> (**CROWD** *reactions.*)

> (*As* **ANNOUNCER** *speaks,* **EDIE**, *dressed as the Liberty Bell, runs out from the back room and takes a gun belt and Colt .45 from the wall.*)

> (*One of the phones on the table rings – it's hers. She picks it up and talks into it as she runs out the door.*)

EDIE. DJFDALKFJKDJFDLJF?

ANNOUNCER. *(Voice-over.)* Look! At the top of the hill, coming from the museum! Is that Benjamin Franklin and Betsy Ross? God Bless America! Ben and Betsy show no fear! They're charging the Brits' front line!

> (*The band begins a spirited version of "Yankee Doodle."*)

Look at the Liberty Bell! She's armed and sprinting toward the Brit football game! Wait! What is Cornwallis pulling out of that trunk? Cornwallis is firing paintballs!

> (**JESS** *runs back in carrying a British flag, hat, and a dozen wallets that she dumps on the table. She grabs a World War II machine gun and runs back out.*)

ANNOUNCER. *(Voice-over.)* Ben is back and he means business! Liberty's sprinting toward King George! Look at those moves!

CROWD. *(Voice-over.)* GO BELL, GO BELL, GO BELL!

> (**ANN**, *covered with different colors of paint, runs in and grabs a sword from the wall just as* **LOUISA** *comes out of the back room as George Washington and* **HESTER** *as Martha. All stop at the door, looking out.*)

HESTER.	**ANN.**	**LOUISA.**
EDIE!	STOP!	OH NO!

ANNOUNCER. *(Voice-over.)* I can't believe my eyes! This is our best battle ever! The Liberty Bell takes down King George with a flying tackle!

HESTER. That's Humphrey Hodkins under Edie!

ANN. They're wrestling!

LOUISA. That's not wrestling.

> *(They run to join the fray.)*

ANNOUNCER. *(Voice-over.)* And now a word from our sponsors: After a hard day at war, there's nothing a soldier wants more than a trim and soothing massage. Cutiecles Nail Salon knows that, and they're offering a fifty percent discount for Battle of New Bunion veterans. Make sure your Fourth has a happy ending. You've served your country, now let Cutiecles serve you.

> (**JESS** *runs in, covered in dirt, gets behind the cannon, and pushes it out the door.*)

Two redcoats have Betsy Ross in a headlock! Now they are piling on Martha!

> (**JESS** *runs back in for the fire extinguisher.*)

Look at George wailing on those nancy boys!

CROWD. *(Voice-over.)* GO! GO! GO! GO!

ANNOUNCER. *(Voice-over.)* The Brits are pulling the Liberty Bell off King George!

(Sounds of gunshots.)

Remember kids, this is not real blood! This is living history!

> *(**EDIE**, with a torn costume, runs in, puts the teeth back in the bear, grabs the hairball, and exits.)*

Martha and Betsy are up! Look at Betsy swing her bunting! They're coming at the British from all sides! Look at that! Can that be a three-point mock flanking maneuver?

> *(Sounds of gunshots.)*

The Brits have opened fire again! Is that Benjamin Franklin behind that cannon? It is! What is the Liberty Bell loading into its chamber? Look at that! Who knew George Washington could box? And check out that finishing move by Martha.

> *(Explosion of cannon, a man's scream. **CROWD** gasps.)*

King George has been hit with a hairball! Oh, the humanity! Franklin and Betsy Ross are pushing the cannon past the front line! The British are running! The British are running!

> *(Marching band music picks up tempo.)*

Now the band is chasing them!

> *(Sound of bus horn blast.)*

And here come our patriots on a bus courtesy of the Board of Education!

> *(Cheers and whistles. An exhausted **LOUISA**, **ANN**, **EDIE**, **HESTER**, and **JESS** enter the museum, holding on to each other for support. Covered with grass, wearing about half their costumes, and out of breath.)*

The Tories have turned tail! For yet another year America has won the Battle of New Bunion! Let's give three cheers for the spunky patriots of the New Bunion Historical Society!

(The CROWD cheers three times.)

EDIE. *(To JESS.)* You shot General Cornwallis!

JESS. He was acting!

LOUISA. He was bleeding!

ANN. *(To EDIE.)* What were *you* doing with King George?

EDIE. I tackled Humphrey Hodkins and he wouldn't let go of me! He had me in a lip-lock!

JESS. Awesome!

EDIE. Not awesome! He was kissing me because he thought I was a guy!

ANN. I'm sorry, Edie. You must feel terrible.

EDIE. I do. But it taught me something. I'll never love from afar again. The next time I see a man I like, I'm going to walk right up to him and say, "Hey, Mister – break me off a piece of that."

ANN. *(With effort.)* Louisa. I'm sorry. We did steal your teeth.

HESTER. I'm even sorrier for how my family treated you, beginning to end. We've always thought we're the biggest deals in New Bunion.

EDIE. You're still its biggest liars.

JESS. I'm the one who took the teeth. They only found out right before you walked in. I thought it would help them and it wouldn't hurt you.

(EDIE walks over to the bear head, takes the teeth from the mouth, crosses, and hands them to LOUISA.)

ANN. Call the police or whatever you need to do.

(ANN leans the Betsy Ross flag against the wall.)

HESTER. We're closing our doors. Everything we're built on is a falsehood.

LOUISA. A lot of it, yes. But admitting it's a first step.

(She takes the flag and puts it back in its base.)

Do you remember what John Adams said when the war was over? "Forgiveness doesn't change the past –"

HESTER. "But it does enlarge the future. Let us bear in mind that as the sword was the last resort for the preservation of our liberties, so it ought to be the first thing laid aside when those liberties are firmly established."

LOUISA. Exactly.

HESTER. But George Washington said it.

LOUISA. *(Ready to contradict her.)* George…

(Thinks.)

You're right.

ANN. She is?

LOUISA. Yes, she is.

*(Hands the teeth to **ANN**.)* You can have them for Black History Month. The one in February.

*(To **HESTER**.)* I better hear you danced your ass off. Now, I've got a long ride to Washington.

ANN. When you get there? I'd have someone at the Smithsonian look closely at your Jefferson miniature.

LOUISA. Why's that?

ANN. I don't have my tools to be sure, but I think your restorer defrauded you. You said he removed the sediment covering it?

LOUISA. Yes.

ANN. The artist's signature isn't clear because it's not totally cleaned, like the rest of it. I think it's a forgery. Your restorer kept the authentic portrait and gave you back a counterfeit.

LOUISA. How would you know this?

ANN. That's what I do. Restore Art.

HESTER. Louisa? Would you ever consider joining our Historical Society? It might be time we made some changes here.

EDIE. Three hundred years late.

LOUISA. Thank you, Hester. But I don't think so.

ANNOUNCER. *(Voice-over.)* We have a news bulletin: Mayor Ronald Rice has just been arrested for accepting bribes from the Canine Olympics Committee to build the Doggy Water Park.

HESTER, ANN & EDIE. YES!

ANNOUNCER. *(Voice-over.)* It looks like we'll be having early elections.

JESS. That's it!

ANN. What?

JESS. Politics! It's the next logical step! I'm running for mayor!

ANNOUNCER. *(Voice-over.)* After today's great turnout, the Reenactment Committee is thrilled to announce the Civil War is coming to New Bunion! This Labor Day the Union and the Confederacy will meet on this hillside to fight the Battle of Bunion Hill led by General George Patton, Davy Crockett, and special guest Harriet Tubman driving our new Husky 3 fire truck!

*(Cheers from the **CROWD**.)*

LOUISA. Let me think about joining your board.

HESTER. Why don't we host a real reenactment? George Washington coming to New Bunion for James Tye to make his teeth?

ANN. We can recreate our town in 1773. The Bunions, the Tyes, the birth of Louisa. We'll actually present what really happened.

LOUISA. Another thing that happened? James Tye went to fight with Washington. Because in 1774, Sampson Bunion freed all his slaves...according to the new Quaker Doctrine. After the war, the town welcomed him back a hero. I don't know if it was because he fought for his country or they needed a blacksmith. Maybe both. I'll get the miniature if you wouldn't mind taking another look.

ANN. I'm happy to.

EDIE. Oh!

> *(To* **ANN.***)* I forgot this after I was manhandled. For at least three minutes. Maybe more. My shop called. I had asked them to look through our records. We keep copies of all our deliveries. I think Jayden must have screwed up and used us instead of another flower delivery.

ANN. I don't understand.

EDIE. Your husband sent his yoga instructor a six-hundred-dollar orchid delivery. WITH a message card: "Dear Yogini, tonight I will Shiva your Shakti. Your Downward Dog, Ruff."

JESS. That's pretty disgusting, but what's the big deal?

EDIE. He sent this in January. A month before their separation. So, he was already Shiving her Shakti. It violates his prenup agreement. Ann's entitled to as big a settlement as she can squeeze out of him.

> *(***ANN*** says nothing; she seems lost in thought.)*

HESTER. Ann? Are you all right?

ANN. Yes, I am. I'm just thinking our museum needs a new wing.

> *(The women react in agreement.)*

EDIE. No more *Jeopardy* for me. Tonight I'm going to happy hour and watching *Shark Tank*.

HESTER. I'm going home to google "Kansa."

ANN & EDIE. "Kwanzaa"!

> *(Sound of fireworks and the band playing.***)*

LOUISA. Happy Independence Day.

HESTER. Happy Independence Day.

> *(The women walk to the door, watching the sky lighting up. To the tune of "America*

---

*A license to produce *George Washington's Teeth* does not include a performance license for any third-party or copyrighted music. Licensees should create an original composition or use music in the public domain. For further information, please see Music Use Note on page 3.

> *the Beautiful,"* **HESTER** *begins to sing "New Bunyon's Town Song.")*

HESTER.
> NEW BUNION DAY
> NEW BUNION DAY
>> *(**EDIE** joins in.)*

HESTER & EDIE.
> WE RAISE OUR VOICE TO THEE
>> *(**ANN** and **JESS** join.)*

HESTER, EDIE, ANN & JESS.
> FOR SAMPSON BUNION'S LEADERSHIP
>> *(**LOUISA** joins.)*

ALL.
> AND HIS FERTILITY
> NEW BUNION DAY, NEW BUNION DAY
> OUR HOME SO STRONG AND FREE
> WITH HAND IN HAND WE TAKE OUR STAND
> AND CLAIM OUR HISTORY.
>> *(Final fireworks, lights fade. Blackout.)*

End of Play

www.ingramcontent.com/pod-product-compliance
Lightning Source LLC
Chambersburg PA
CBHW050303010526
44108CB00040B/2252